Deep Wonder

Christmas Journey

Love like electricity
Lights through his hands
From Christ to us
Stars to self …

Deep Wonder

Poems by
Philip C. Kolin

Grey Owl Press

Grey Owl Press
P.O. Box 5334
Takoma Park MD 20913-5334
http://www.greyowlpress.com

Design and typography by Tomoko Hirata, Design Studio TMK
Cover photo by Al Levine
Illustrations by Christopher J. Pelicano, A.R.T. Services
Printed by Reproductions, Inc.

ISBN 0-9671901-1-8
Library of Congress Card Number: 00-107517

Also available from Grey Owl Press:
Lion Sun: Poems by Pavel Chichikov, ISBN 0-9671901-0-X

∞ The paper used in this publication meets the minimum requirements of the
American National Standard for Information Sciences—Permanence of Paper for
Printed Library Materials, ANSI Z39.48-1984.

Contents

The Banquet of Christ

Bravissimo, Abba!

End Time

Jesus in Gethsemane
Prayed a rosary
Blood red
Each bead
A century of love …

Preface

The poems in this book stem from the most difficult time of my life. A beloved fiancée suddenly walked out of my life, with no explanation, no warning. I was shaken to my foundations. Losing someone whom I loved so deeply, someone I thought felt the same way about me, sent me into a desert, a state of panic alternating with numbness of heart and spirit. I had taken love for granted. When it was gone, I felt abandoned. If you have ever lost someone essential to your happiness, you know the feeling: the rejection and the fear, dreams turned into dust.

I began praying, deeply, daily, hoping that God would restore my fiancée — and with her, purpose, hope, and promise. A close friend and Episcopal priest, Father Ed Lundin, told me one night that my heart had been broken so that God could open it. My spiritual mother, Margie Parish, a woman of powerful faith and enormous love for me, led me to Scripture and deepened my prayer life in innumerable ways. Knowing that I had written poetry before, Margie told me that if I only obeyed and listened to God, He would whisper love poems to me.

For years I had promised God that I would write a book of love poems just for Him. But I had put off fulfilling the promise, concentrating instead on my academic career. I had published more than 20 books and 160 scholarly articles. I wrote a religious poem here and there, and I even devoted a third of a book of otherwise secular poems, published in 1994, to religious topics. I thought I was giving God the credit for my written work, but He wanted (and deserved) the substance.

When I desperately needed love, God filled my emptiness with His very self. God sent Himself to help me keep a promise that He Himself fulfilled. God is both the origin and the completion of this volume.

Each night I prayed, with tears, with trust, and with hope that my fiancée would come back to me. The more I prayed, the more God asked me to write about love, but love for Him. He told me that He was the desire of my heart. If I would go to my kitchen table and write what He whispered to me, I would have the promise and consolation of a love greater than anything on earth. These poems are God's gift to me; they are the miracle of His love. They are His words, not mine. I am merely His scribe.

In the course of a hundred days, these poems were sent to me. They are the markers of a journey I took to and with God, but a journey He had planned, mapped, scripted, and completed. I learned about God the Poet of the Universe. I found that the Poet God is the Word made words. I saw in His poems Christ my lover — not a substitute for love, but the restorer of it.

Some of these poems came in a minute or two; others evolved over a night of prayer. But all of them speak of God's constancy, His steadfast love. My prayer is that God will whisper to you just as He did to me as you take your journey to Him through these poems. Blessed be God.

Philip C. Kolin

Lent 1999

We Two Are More

We two are more
Gathered together
In these lines
You and me
My words holding
Your eyes, your eyes
Holding my words
Embraced in one
Corinthian love.

In our midst
Of these syllables
Comes Christ
The Word for
The words I write;
You read; we pray.

Let's petition
Him for each other
Right now.

I lift you up
To Him, In Him
Through Him here
To perfect in you
What He is doing
In me, please see
Glory around us

Rejoice: all
The blank, white
Emptiness of our lives
He is filling
Dwelling here with
His Word.

Glory to God.

The Desert

Kneeling

*The quickest way
To ascend the stairs
To the throne
Is to kneel …*

The Desert

Lord, you called me
Into the desert
When I thought
Things were going
So well; love was
Mine for the making
Soft honey
Safe selfishness.

I fell into
A wasteland of
Loneliness—
Hope died next
Buried in
A field of cactus
Tombstones.
Each step I took
Scorpion doubt
Stinging me,
A festering sore
That got worse
The more I journeyed.
You gave me one option
Alone: the desert.

I prayed about
When I got out
For getting out
Was the reason
I thought I
Was in.

I cried out
For any earthly
Signatory of love.
Sought every savor

Of a touch.
You kept even the wind
From caressing me.
I would have made
Advances to the lizards of lust
If I thought
They would kiss
Me with their grooved tongues
But even these
You tamed into
Scurrying submission
To you.

I covered myself
In hairy worry
Ate wild excuses
Was drugged
On wormwood memories
Repeated acts of
Impotent desire.

I exclaimed
To ghosts.
Who can argue
From nothing?
The rhetor's
Folly lies.
I kept an appointment
Book of dates
On calendars of dust.
I wrote billets doux
In torment.

I kept fantasy
Alive in fleshly dreams
That carry the weight
Of dry wind.

I calculated
Each day's accumulation
Nothing in which to place
Nothing.
Not even sand fleas
Propagate.
Multiplicity is subtraction
In your desert, Lord.

The sun which
Burned me raw
Healed me eternally.

I feasted on
Your paradoxes:
The less I struggled
The more I was free.

Surrender is victory.
Desert is desire aright.

My desert of Calvary
Ended in your arms
Outstretched
Succoring me with
The manna of Yourself.
Amen.

Where Am I, Lord?

Lord,
Where am I
In your plan
Am I just
Starting out
Pushing off

Or am I
In the middle
Halfway
On the journey
Half right
Perhaps
Half wrong
Help me, Lord
Or am I
Near the end
Finishing
What you
Started
For me?

Marriages Made in Heaven

Father, hear the
Wounds my heart
Makes when
Others slash
My hopes for love.

Too many times
Father, a lover
Has promised
Me the happiness
Of a sunset life
But left at dawn
Or before the darkness
I could not see.

Why, God, do lips
Tender with passion's
Hallowed promise
Speak hollow
Conceited covenants?

Why must love
Always be a competition for
Winning the greatest hurt?

Jesus, you were
And are as we
So you know
The surprise of agony
The kiss that was
The cross that is.
What must I do
To be like you
Must all the dates
Of my life
Be made at Calvary?
Can't one
Lead to Cana?

His voice answered:
Empty yourself
Assume a slave's courtship
Of bended humility
Lay your heart down
Pride first
Bless all widows
Abandoned spouses
Jilted brides
Hapless daughters
And then listen
The Father of Love
Will start calling
Couples before His altar
Your turn will come
When the least of you expects it.

Close

Jesus, hold me
Close today
The world
Is too empty

I need closure.

Shepherd my heart
A lost stray
In the confines
Of your pinfold.

Close your
Loving hands
Around my life

Lock the gates
After I'm in.
Eternity is time's
Enclosure with you.

Lord Shepherd

He is Lord Shepherd
Of all the flock
Of your cares, doubts,
Self-betrayals.
His pasture is
Your heart
Fertilized by faith.
Ask Him for rain
To turn wilderness words
Of no hope, no hope
Into verdant prayers.

At dawn He rises
Surrounded by the mist
Of the Holy Spirit
The first sign of the cross
All day He enlightens
Amid any darkness within
His crozier comforts
Like a father's compliment.

He shepherds best
In the desert
Not a sheep dies
Perishing from thirst
From His careful flock.
He carries an oasis
Inside His heart
To water seedless sand:
Here is where your verdant
Prayers bloom in the desert.

Christ's Investment

Christ, the world
Wants me to be
For sale, cheap, easy
I am listed
On so many
Cut-rate markets,
Slashed, discounted.

On some days
I fear all my stock
Is good only
To be traded
Off to the lowest
Bid: depreciation.

But I know that you
Reverse the world's
Market: you buy me
At a great price
And pay it once again
In love and mercy
When my worth
Is down in the world.

Lord, I'm glad
I am in your
Company tonight.

Unhook Me, Father

Come tonight, Father
Healer of all hurts
Binder of wounds
So deep, so lasting
They have gone
Into my future
With tentacles.

Unhook me, Father
Fisherman, free me
From all those
Catches, lines, bobs
The leaden reproaches
That plummet me away
From your sunlight.

Dress me now
Father in your
Promise so that
I can throw off the
Tattered dreams

That cover me
Like so many
Frayed rags.

Give me the alms
Of the generous King
Christ who frees me
From the biting
Sores of beggars' ticks.

Make me new,
Whole, start
My life over
The way you
Knew it would
When you
Created me fresh
An eternity ago.

Goodnight, Abba

Goodnight, Abba
I know it's always
Light where you are
But down here
I'm in the dark
And curtained fears
Are covering
The windows of my eyes
Can't your Son
Rise earlier this
Morning in my soul?

Tuck me in
Tonight as well
As you did

Tomorrow's yesterday
Time is all one
For you.

Hear my night
Prayers, Father:
I struggle
With alarmed clocks
The panic of
My mortality.
Please forgive me.

I will rest
Better knowing you
Wrap me in
The comfort of
Your Word:
The kindness
That makes us
All your favorites.
Thanks for keeping
Your family album—
The Bible—
 Close to my bed.

Thanks for leaving
The night lights
Of heaven on
The stars…
Their twinkle
Sounds like
The laughter of
Your gentle Fatherhood

Goodnight, Abba
If I call out
Tonight I know you

Are always up
To hold me
Close to you
And will anoint
All my fears with
The light of your love.

Boost Me, God

Boost me, God
Up from the shadows
Where I struggle
With darkened reflections
Of what I think
I should be.

Take my hand
Into the light
Where I can see me
As clearly as you
Do without critical dust
Clouding the view.

Show me, Lord
What you want
Me to do with
This beam of life
You have carved
Out of existence
Only for me.

Lord, my spirit is
Disabled, crippled
By expectations
I never met
You never sent.

I hobble on
In a life
I wear out with
Hope-bare complaints
Tearing at your heart.

Lord, hear me
Cry for you
In all those times
I long for accomplishments
That never are seen
When you have
Already pictured me
Whole and fitting
In your perfect sight.

Surrender

Cast aside
Any worry
That hooks
You to doubt

Let your soul
Surrender
All that
You are
And will
Be to Him

He can
Create
An Eve
Or an atom
A star
Or a starfish

He is
Lord over
All.

Christt Is Light

All the guilt
We carry inside
Prepares us for
Refuge in the world's
Failure dump.

Our souls become
Oppressed with
Milestones of
Self recriminations
We engrave
Our hearts
With burdens
Of the past—
Living tombstones
Long before
We die.

Christ is light
He bears
A creation load
Of dark, heavy
Crosses to heaven
Nothing weighs
Him down
Except the
Rubbish of
Our refusal
To let Him.

God's Scales

Under the canopy
Of heaven
The Father measures
All our days
Weighing the graces
He sends us
On a scale
Balanced by
Our obedience.

God tips
His side
Of the scale
Down to us
Raising our desires
High enough
To touch Heaven's doorknob
But just when
We are close
Enough to turn it
We start loading
Our end of the scale
With all of the
World's claims to know:
Ponderous pride's self justifications
Brocaded pain masquerading as gain
Fear we are not doing well
Here below
We fall
Keeping God's
Graces up in the air.

All grains of yes
Can make our end
Of the scale light:
Kneeling prayer

Trusting leaps of
Faithful surrender
Patient hearts
Resting in love

All of these
Spiritual weights
Of the soul
Make the scale
Go out of our control
Sending us flying
Up to heaven
As God's graces
Plummet down
To us.

God's rule of thumb:
He measures not
By how heavy
Our heart is
In the world
But by how light
Our spirit is
In Him.

Cast Out Your Fears

Shake the dust of disbelief
From your eyes and
Go before the whole world
With the mark of resurrection.
Let the water of your baptism
Be a glowing river of
Light: signs and wonders.

Cast out the devils of
Dark world despair
Withering away dumb…
Make a way for
Faith to bloom
In the glorious tongues
Of the Good News
He spoke: you heard.

Don't be afraid
To pluck up
By the roots
The snake-like
Threats that lie
Like honest doubts
In men's fearful hearts:
Show the world
What the darkness
Has concealed
From their light.

No poison will
Swallow your words
But instead they
Will multiply into
Hospices of hope
For all the sick
Depending on the
Gospel of your hands
Anointed by
The Lord of recovery.

Christ's Hospital

Christ's hospital
Has open admissions
Grace for balm
Kisses for pain
Hugs for broken
Souls and hearts.

His wards are all
Those places His people
Wander wounded
He is the Red Cross
Shepherd; the compassionate
Medic of the Father
Going across every
Battlefield
Anointing every cry
Refusing no casualty
Even after death
He is the gurney of
The lost.

Christ's anesthesia
Is prayer
Deadening desolation
Soothing hope
The sleep of the sick
Unction to all
Those burned by
The world's contagion:
Prayer is the holy
Quarantine of recovery.

His Sacred Heart is
The medicine chest
Of the universe
Transfusing cures
Through His precious blood.

Christ's pharmacopeia
Are the words of Scripture
He is the prescription
Dispensing parables—
Take three a day
For life.

His emergency room
Is busiest whenever
Your heart aches
So deeply
You need His love
To heal the rupture.

Kneeling

The quickest way
To ascend the stairs
To the throne
Is to kneel
Low and on
The hardest, uneven ground.

Seek ye not
The kingdom of comfort
But the place
Where you are halved
In pride
But doubled in spirit.

Let Him know
That you are legless
On the journey to Him
Measuring distances in Aves
Not leaping avenues
He will speed you on
Your way in prayer.

A kneeling soul
Gets Christ's perspective
Of the world:
A dwarfed race
Compared to the
Towering majesty of all creation
Yet the glory of its Maker.

Amen.

Ascend

Let His light
Burst inside you
Spreading its fire
All through your
Artery runways

Feel it empower
All the flights
Your eyes make
Toward Him in others.

Then watch: you'll
Ascend the ground
Less fears
Into an orbit
Of grace all
Around your heart.

The Gardener of the Universe

Lilies need shadows
To grow beautiful
In the dark they
Are readied for
The light of healing.

We are impatient
Gardeners who toil
More in loud worry
Than in quiet wonder.

Let your Heavenly Father
Prepare you
Plot your days
Plant your ways
Prune your excesses
Frustrating His harvest.

The Gardener of the Universe
Blesses the smallest
Seeds of trust
While thrashing
Overwrought passionflowers,
Unfulfilling promise.

Poor Boxes

So many hearts
Are like the church
Poor boxes
Protected in obscurity
From real generosity
Hidden in a corner
Or sealed small
In a wall.

They attract notice
Only from those
Whose grace is gratitude.
The world that forgets
Drops a penny's worth
Of time and care
Satisfying the motion
Of the hand but not
The glory of the vow.

Those who place
The tender society
Values most highly
Gain with giving
Come close to the
Carpenter's son's
Blueprint for salvation.

He builds
Poor boxes
The size of cathedrals
All around the
Globe of heaven.

Amen.

Forgiveness

Forgive those who trespass
Against your heart,
A hard lesson to taste
Bitter with injury
Flavored memory.

But each time you forgive
Your memory is baptized
Anew with sweet rainbows.

Your heart will dine
At the Father's feast
On leavened hope
And turtle dove peace.

He will give you
One of His spiced
Kisses for your love
At His communion table.

A Photograph from Heaven

Imagine a photograph
Taken in heaven
And then shown
Here on earth
The wonder, the majesty
Columns of rejoicing
In a temple of voices.
Can this be possible?
No, no.

The photograph is
Available: now, today
Just close the
Shutter of your eyes
And let the sight
You see stay
A moment or two
Then you'll behold
The image of God
Taken by your heart
And developed
In your spirit.

The closer you are
To Him the quicker
The negative will
Turn positive
Light all around.

Here's the photograph
He sent to you
From heaven today
Close your eyes:
Smile for another.

Abba Father

Who can say
God is unseen
Absconded in a cloud
Or in a hidden voice
Shutting His people
Out of touch?

I have seen Him
Bountiful times today
In ways as soft
As a whispered kiss
Or as outgoing
As a reunion of hugs.

He is resurrected
In each smile.
I've sketched His
Sight in faces
That welcome
Trust when doubt
Pays a greater
Worldly dividend.

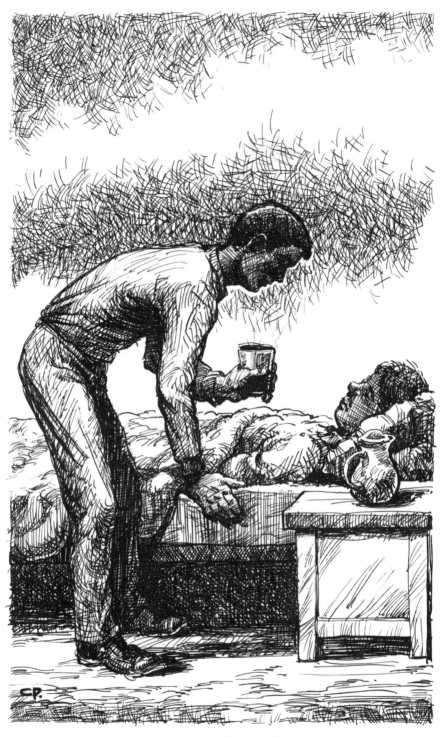

Abba Father

*I have seen Him
Bountiful times today …*

He works at the
Blood bank
For strangers.
He's made Capernaum
And Hattiesburg twin cities
Each time kindly sunlight
Blesses a cure with saving hope
At a hospital room,
Nursing home,
Or marriage counselor's.

God's posture is
Not always erect
And sublime
That's His heavenly gait
But on earth He enters
Laughing arthritic hands
Faithful arrhythmic hearts
Or wheezing lungs
That sing out alleluias
On a respirator.

He ate dinner today
With all those hungry families
Whose fathers have left
Mothers to feed
Children alone
On two jobs and love
A day, a long day.

God's tears fell
Like Galilee rain
When the abortion clinic
Added a new wing:
A dove fell
For a raven to soar.

In memories of love
He dances with us
To quicken our step
Closer to Him.
Turn the most
Beautiful room
Of your house—
Your soul—
Into an echo
Chamber for
His love songs.

Amen.

A Eucharist Holiday

God carries a knapsack
Filled with a picnic
For all His children's souls.

He packs all
The good things
He knows we need
As well as graces
We can't imagine.

He calls us
To the outing of our lifetime—
A day in the
Country of God's heart.

He positions the sun
Just right: in the sky
Spreads the winds so
They don't blow or blast
Fragrances the air
To relish us.

On a sun-filled knoll
Atop the valley of life
He prepares a
Banqueting table
Covered with a
Checkered cloth
Of red and white.

Angels help Him
Serve us
His own
Flesh and blood:
Jesus.

God Be My Prayer

God be my prayer
Book for life
Turn my eyes
Into holy hands
Furrowing across
Your harvest pages
Reaping me into
Your living Word
Fruitful in all
Seasons and ages.

Through chapters
And verses
Run my course
Until you become
The prize of my heart.

Stop me, O Lord,
When midway you
Want to anoint

My touch, your blessing
Reserved for that day
My day in you.

Script your own
Servant, Lord
In your style
So that I read
Like your new book:
The Letter to the Americans.

Maranatha

Lord, I do not think
Your favor anchors
Those who navigate
Into a negotiated eternity
With comfortable births
Pious piers
Yachting into
Harbored glory.

I trust, Lord, that
You stroll
The more stormy seas
Of daily life
With their pitching cares
And doubts and cares
Keelhauling us
Until we
Squalling vessels
Are Christened calm
By your holy love.

The present is your
Mooring time.
Now your Maranatha flows.

Come!

The call to glory
Is a life
Finely tuned
Not to the
Decibels of doubt
But the softness
Of smiles in
The midst of alarms.

Don't let
Christ find you
Deaf to the quiet
Resurrections He
Is planning for you.

His way of
Reaching His
People across
Centuries or
Stanzas

Is easy
And short:
Come!

Jesus Ministers

Christ, The King of Doors

His love is a door
That opens even
When we try to close
It …

Christ, the King of Doors

Welcome Christ
The King of Doors
In your life.

Let Him have
Control of all
The handles
And knobs
You try to
Turn furiously
For your good.

Let Him open
Or close
As He sees
Fit for you.

His love is a door
That opens even
When we try to close
It. Our selfishness
Cannot keep
Him out

A closed door
Here below
Does not always
Mean you are
Locked out

He may be
Shutting one
Door to open
Another better one
For all eternity.

Don't leave
Any of His doors
Ajar with
Stubborn complaints—
You could stand
In the way of
A miracle.

Put your trust
Not a doubting hand
In the gash in His side:
The door He opened
To close you
In His heart forever.

Amen.

Inside Christ

Inside Christ
There are shepherds
Fields white with sheep.
Fig trees
Grow out of wells
Flowing streams of air
Swell into rivers
Lilies of the field
Are watered until
They blossom into clouds.

All the Old and the New
Testaments for faith
Unfold like a cavalcade
Of marching armies
Of lovers
Leap forward

Within Christ
Every prayer ever
Said at any time
Grows fertile
Flowering in Him:
God's perfect will

All the hurts of time
Are cradles in His heart
Nursed into eternal hope
Christ's heart is
The door to heaven.
Open it when you
Hear it knock
Inside you.

Christmas Journey

His journey begins
Inside out
Conception to
Crucifixion
Timelessness to trust
Let communion banners
Fly over us
In a Eucharist parade
This Hallowedmass.

Heaven's King
Comes today
On all the lips
Of those who
Praise Him.
Our lips are
Echoes to the
Silent sounds of majesty
Imperfect kisses

In a love affair
To be consummated
Another way.

Sun light the night
Tonight, this night
God's child
Wrapped in flesh
A present for
All our futures.

Right now see
God touches Christ
The way a father
Might at confirmation
Or a bar mitzvah.
Love like electricity
Lights through His hands
From Christ to us
Stars to self.

The glory of His coming
Opens roads in rivers
Waterfall journeys into
Fonts filled with holy tears
Gifts of the Spirit
To the faithful
To purify their eyes
In a world only
To look for Him.

Every Gloria starts
A blade of hope
Growing green
Deep inside us
Planting God's
Holy holly:
Christ within.

Mary's Covenant

In Nazareth a young
Milkmaid so graced
With a fruitful heart
Said Yes in a
World accustomed to no

But did not
While she did.

Her knowledge placed
The world at the end
Of God's love
The farthest reach
Of His hand made
Into earth.

Her Yes was heard
Across the centuries
And the galaxies
It was the sign above
The cross of love.

O Mary conceived
In the heart of the Father
And espoused by the Spirit
Cradle your Son tonight
In a world aborting life
In the middle of love.

Before time started
Its pace through
The vale of fears
Mary's Yes echoed
The plans of Architect God's
Creation. She is

The Mater for His troweling
Sky, moon, and sun

The Father's favorite
Daughter on earth
Carried a basket
Of crosses
Laced with honey
Perfume and pain.

The fruit from Mary's
Garden filled a universe
With stars, for Christ, twinkling
The paths for
Wisemen and willing virgins
Husbands who sleep with
Their wives in Christ
Sarah, Ruth, Gomer, Elizabeth.
All wait for—
And we are still
Waiting for—
The Messiah
She conceived
In her basket
Decorated with
Royal arcs,
Ribbons blue.

See now
Today Christ
Descending into
Mary
Christmas

Sanctus Bells

Natural laws
Of water, ice
Air, wind
Sun, sight
Are happily undone
To be redone
At the sound
Of the Sanctus
Bells ringing,
Ringing, praying.

Across the conscience
Of continents
And centuries
All of us dancing
At the communion of
Saints are anointed
In sound, making
Us holy thurifers
Incense as sweet
As Bethlehem polyphony.

Sanctus bells
Ring out
Each time
An angel
Gives a child
A guardian's gift
Of holiness
On Christmas Day
Gravity surrenders
Its dull predictability
So a universe
Pregnant with joy
Can be born
Into the cradle
Of the Father's bosom.

The gift of grace
Is that God
Transfers the
Sounds all around
Us into us
While the Lord of All
Harmony's harmony
Plays a melody of
Himself into
The composition—
A sound recording
The Song of Songs.

The Prodigal's Brother

Look at the prodigal
His story and his brother's
Both belong to the same Father
Sprung from the same root of love
Sat at His table, shared
All the fruits, the promise
Yet the prodigal received
The better share, though equally
Divided between the brothers.

The brother ate the bitter
Fruit of lost time
That could have been his gain
He wanted merit
The Father gave mercy.
He chose to proclaim
A steady history
Of work, schedules
The Father rewarded
One bright moment of yes
From sorrow-filled lips.

The brother works still
A lot of motion
But little warmth
In his busyness
He has no time
For others' pain
He has no tolerance
For late arrivals,
Tearful regrets.

But the prodigal
Reclines in Father Abraham's
Bosom, enjoying
The Fruit of the Vine.

The Anointing of Lazarus

Come out of your tombs
Throw off the death cloth
Of defeat, doom, despair.

Your tomb might be
An office where calumny
Is bought and sold
In a marketplace of deceit.

Or your tomb may be
A church where back-
Biting and harping
Sing slander willfully
In the choir of shadows

Maybe your tomb
Is a marriage
Dead to love because
Cheating selfishness

Has buried vows under
A headstone pillow.

Your tomb might be
Your body tormented
With festering doubts
And loss of esteem
You might be bonded
A slave to the commerce
Of pride, looks, cash.

Your city might be
Another, larger tomb
Overtaxing residents
With corpulent vice
Trafficking in
Drugs, pollution
For soul and mind.

Don't let time
Be the tomb
That traps you,
Suffocating you out of
Devotion, prayer,
Or other life-
Giving freedoms
In a dictatorship
Of clocked consumption.

Lord Jesus Christ
Physician to the entombed
We ask you now for
The anointing of Lazarus

Let your Word
Raise all those
Fallen dead asleep

Set your alarm
Of hope to wake
Us up to life
In You
Beautiful and
Abundant.

Mark 2

Lord, how often
Do we crowd
You out
With lame complaints
Against your Word

Summon the four
Archangels, Charioteer
Of the wind, the Holy Spirit
To lower our
Paralytic souls
Right in your midst
Dwelling in your Sacred Heart.

Calm us with your
Forgiving touch
Let us know that
It is only inside you
That God redeems offenses
With the healing authority
Of His gentle love.

Lord, tell us to
Pick up all
The stretchers on which
We lie with sin, doubt,
Betrayal, the infirmities of faith

And to go home
Waiting there for you;

Order us to run
So all can see
Us praising God
On our way
We pass the putrefied
Seated scribes
Who never rose
To the light of truth
That you came
In their midst, too,
With cures for their
Crippled souls,
Halting unforgiveness.

Women at the Well

The line of women
At Jacob's well
Was seeking, longing
A taste, touch of
The Christ: Light.

Magdalene had to go
In seven times
She was baptized
From worldly thirst
With the waters
Of living life.

The little girl
Lay at the bottom
Of the synagogue

Dead by law
Risen to life
By flowing love.

The Samaritan wife,
Pailing for husbands,
Clutched a sterile mountain
At the bottom of the well…
He showed her Jerusalem
In the fullness of His smile.

Women today should
Return to the well
Their wombs would
Harvest, not abort,
What He soweth
They need to labor
Reaping lives
For eternity.

Luke 5:1–11

Lord, lower your nets
Into all those empty
Lakes we fish for in spite
Of catching only darkness

And prickly shadows.
Haul out your dry catch
Remove all the hooks,
Coiled lies strangling
Us in scheduled slime.
Speak us unraveled
With your Word.

Put us out into the deep
Light up to our breaking
Point. Then cast into us
The dazzling sight of You
Fishing with Zebedee

Looking for more sons
To help in the day's catch

On shore I drop my lines

Sunset Vision

In sunsets
God paints salvation
On a canvas of sky
Grace and the sight to see it:
Earth and heaven reconciled.

The pure white host
Of God's glory
Is a transfiguration
Too bright for more
Than a moment's doxology
Too sharp, piercing
At noon, God's holy hour,
For modern apostles.

But a sunset
Is a holy communion—
God hangs His
Dazzling eternity in
The closet of heaven
And robes Himself
In the mantle of humanity—
Its arc

Across the sky
A paten for our eye
To receive the gift.

As you look
See the passion of His love
Stinging red, glory gold,
Burnt orange lashes
On the pillory and crucifixion
Side of the sky
But then He stirs in
The majesty of His mercy
Assured azure, new-birth pink.
Saints always wear
Sunset pastel or scarlet
Depending on the
Love or pain
God clothes them in.

Once you start
Watching a sunset
Follow its mystery
All the way
To the light
Of darkness
In the world.

Gethsemane

In a garden of thorns
He suffered a crown
Barbed with pain
To be placed upon
His head, the glory of all
Creation wounded in love.

Around His temples
This crown pierced
The living God
With a mortal sting:
A short-lived death
Born of the Father's
Eternal love
For Him for us.

The blood He shed
In the garden
Watered the rocks
Into crying prayer:
Hosanna in the highest
King of Kings.

He is with us today
In all the gardens
Of our Gethsemanes
He feels the hollow
Crown of desertion
We are forced to wear
When the world
Mocks our love.

He hurts again
For the wounds
We suffer for being
His in kindness
And perseverance
Before a Caiaphas court.

He walks in
Our gardens
When those we trusted
With human perfection
Betray us with a Judas kiss:
Sin is not original.

He feels all
Our thorns—
Divorce, abortion,
Child abuse
Blasphemous cruelty
Burrowing debts—
Watered by our tears
Into a prayer
Of faith in Him.

He is blessing
You right now
For wearing
His stigmata
Inside your heart.

Every time you cry
He bleeds.

Amen.

A Splinter from His Cross

Look inside your
Soul tonight
See if it beats
With love or
Hides in pain,
Recycled remorse.

Search your heart
To see if it is found
Wanting in will
To follow Him
Or is like the
Rich man carrying

A wallet of time—
He could escort
Christ in Capernaum
But not to the
Hill in Jerusalem.

Give Him the glory
Of the moment now
On your second's hand:
Time's smallest sliver
Looks like a
Splinter from His
Cross in your life.

Wear it in love.

End Time

Jesus in Gethsemane
Prayed a rosary
Blood red
Each bead
A century of love
Each decade
A millennium of marvels
On the Father's calendar
With the Son and Spirit
Three mysteries
All time.

When He finished
With the last
Glory Be

That exactly
Was what the
Father records
For all times
Without end
Ending time.

The Pain Below

So much power
Resides in a thorn
A silver missile
A golden needle
That pierces as it
Heals. Those in need
Come to its power
Through passing pain

Which only lasts a
Short life-
Time all eternity is
Continuous.
Joy if only we can
Look beyond the bread
We eat at daily meals
To the loaves and fish
That swim in the
Enthroned firmament—

The seas around
God's galaxy
Teem with life that
Lasts and lasts and lasts
A Trinity of eternities.
Each decision we make for Him
Takes refuge there:

53

Leaping joys
Prancing peace
Galloping glory
With a stately mane
A fluorescent crown
With all thorns
Removed.

The pain below
Rises as incense
To the Heavenly Father
Above all
Here below.

The King's Arbor

Amid a garden
Of tainted fruit
A single sapling
Stood
Not much to look at
Certainly not the
Vintner's pride.

From that sapling
Came neither cherry red
Berries nor purple
Throated grapes.
It just stood.
That was its crown.

When the vintner
Saw the weak
Sapling he said
Cut it down
Make room for better
Stronger growth

My limited land is
No haven
For profitless pleasure.

So he had it cut down
And tossed it
Outside the garden—
Let it blow away
Or kindle some poor
Man's cold fire.

Along the path
Of the vintner's field
Came a noisy column
Of wine-soaked braggarts
Jailors and Roman guards

One of them saw the sapling
And picked it up
A wooden whip
A supple rod
Free punishment

Once at the jail
A new prisoner
Was readied for
Their seasoned mockery
Their peppered deviltry.

He stood
Alone in a row of rowdies
Big-boned Romans
And Hebrew toadies
Bruised and battered
From spit
The color of rancor
At the speed of hate.

The jailor with the
Centurion too
Decided to hold a mock
Coronation; the prisoner
The victim king.

On his head
They raised a
Crown of thicket thorns
And around his shoulders,
A purple, red mantle,
They had nothing
To put into his hands
But pain.

Then the jailor who
Had carried the sapling
Away exclaimed:
No noble scepter
Let's put a splintered
Piece of bark, a rejected
Sapling
We'll have a new roux
A mockery stood
Within a mockery.

So the sapling was fitted
Into Jesus' hands
His reed of office
His majesty on earth.

Alone he stood
An uprooted tree
His only prop
From which grew
A universe of prophecy
Shoots sprouting stars.

Woodworking

In wood
He works:
A fallen apple
Salvation tree
A time-hewn
Cradle in the stable
Babel free
Carpenter's blocks
Fig trees blooming
In sea water
Oars of broken boats
Healed in the storm
A Cross of light
On a crest of Golgotha.

Inside wood
He planes us
Kindled humanity
Tightly shut in
Dry, dark selves.

He has to consume
Us in Holy Ghost fire
To teach us light
And set us free.

We then
Make beautiful
Flambeaux borders
For His
Calvary mansion.

Christ's Wounds

O Sacred Wounds
Of Love Most Holy
Precious balm
Of blood so pure
Let me hide
Myself in thee.

On your lanced
Side let me
Stand in the gap
For all those souls
Being pierced tonight
By the world's
Spite and scandal.

Hold me sweet
Savior suffering
In your arms
Nurse me into charity
With the greatest deed
Of life born to die
To sinful selfishness.

All around your
Two feet, one nailed
On top of the other,
I see you
Walking on
The waves of
The Red Sea
You once and
Now forever again
Have parted
For my safe
Journey home.

Bless the Name

Lord, how many
Crucifixion's wounds
Did you suffer
In a minute
On Calvary?

Jeers, taunts, insults
To your sacred
Face, heart
Body of light
Assaulted by
Blind ears
The tongues
And lips
Of the dark.

How many curses
Pierced your
Canticle-sweet flesh
For the world
To inflict such
Torrents—syllables
Of rancid contempt
Like hissing lashes
Cut
Opening your heart
Even more to love
Those who hurt
To obtain it.

Lord, a minute's gone
By the time it took
To read this
A new, cruel
Tribe of Golgotha
Has wounded your name
With blasphemous tongues

Lord Christ, I was not
There at Calvary
But I am here
Now, today
Let me pour
Some of my own
Words of succor
Into your
Fresh wounds:

Bless the name
Of Jesus
O my soul
Bless His
Precious, holy name!

The Sea Lane Cross

As the century closes
Ports of hope, family
Abandonment alone
Blow across hearts
Like a dry cold wind
Dissolving lifeboats
Like so many loose splinters

A dark light, a freezing
Penumbra clouds like
A morgue sheet
Over those who want
To live, to love, to trust
Stealing their fishing.

There is a way, one
Sea lane is open, free
A path to peace, hope

That will take
Away pain and give
Warm renewal.

It is the cross.
If you feel it
Move you to hot tears
You'll have water
Enough to sail across
The great divide
Of the dark millennium
Into the age of chrismon.

If you feel unchanged
Heartlocked
Keep touching the cross
Until His tears
Dredge you out
Of the desert of despair
And into the river of life.

Amen.

Anima Christi

Near Capernaum
We are all lame
Hobbling blindly
Toward Calvary

But somewhere on
The road
Long before Paul
Was struck with faith
We approach Emmaus.

He talks us down
From our Crosses
Each day we care
To listen to
Our hurts found
In others.

Go forth and teach
All nations to do
Likewise as at Calvary:
Accepting their cross
Ends our torment.

"Sanctificator nomen, Jesu"
The chorus of children sings
Around the Easter candle
Sparkle in the light of
Their resurrected eyes.

The Banquet of Christ

Union

Take me up
With you
Above the orchard clouds …

Christ, My Courtier

He is a suave courtier
My Christ, my lover
He wears a cape
Of seasons
And spreads it out
In the sky
Midnight blue

His ring is
A solitaire—
The moon in
Silver brilliance
Divine.

His suit is
Deep love
Trimmed in
Magenta passion
As soft
As a heartbeat
Waiting for Viaticum

For a boutonniere
He selects
A red sunset
With a stamen
Of stars.

His walking stick
Is a rainbow
Of time and
All the hues
Of creation
Glory in halos
Lighting His step.

His stepfall
Sounds like
The quiet pulsing
Of planets
Making time
In millennia
Not foolish
Minutes.

His smile shines
With sunlight
And across
His laughter
Races the delight
Of does, fulsome
In His pleasure.

Jesus' Proposal to Us

Come all you
Whose hearts
Bear the broken
Bones of human trust
The soot of failure:
The world loves endings.

I love starts
Without finishes
I celebrate bright beginnings
That only get more
Radiant in resurrection—
Time without clocks
Hearts without pain
Promise without pretense
Love without doubt.

My love lasts
Because I am
The one who
Created firsts
That continue
Forever.

I write my vows
In the chronicles of light
In a sky that never
Knows darkness or storm
That showers sunshine
In fine mists refreshing
My beloved people.

In my kingdom of love
All couples are joined
Through me and in me
The Father is their priest
I am the wedding band.

My love flames with
A fire that renews
Discovery and rejoicing
The Paraclete is me
Burning gently within you.
Can you feel His presence
When you say my name?

Heaven's Puppeteer

In an upper room
They saw eternity performed
Simultaneous history
Entire chronicles
In a three-syllable
Prayer: Come, Lord, Come.

He did and does
And wills all
Doing is His being.

The Holy Spirit
Is heaven's
Puppeteer... His strings
The color of sunlight
Tinged with flame
Slide down
To earth
Slaying us
Into power
With His touch.

Here, faithful spectators,
Are the signs of His
Show in us:
Inaudible voices
For us to speak
With tongues on fire
Invisible eyes
For us to read
Between and inside
The lines of God
Opening ears
To the deafeningly
Soft sound of His commands.

As our hands
Extend into the endless
Ineffable air
We are bonded—
Fettered in freedom—
To Him.

Into our souls
He suspends
A light
So preciously radiant
He preserves it
In the tabernacle
Of our hearts.

When the Spirit moves
The light inside us
Dances at the
Feast of the Lamb
In the upper room.

Jesus' Locket

Let your heart
Be His locket
For Him to fill
With joy, more joy.
Allow His picture—
Loving kindness
In others' souls—
To be reflected
Everywhere, yes,
Everywhere
He is the
Mirror Mirrored.

Inside His locket
Place yourself too
Around your neck
Wear it like the cross
Of Calvary but after
Magdalene washed
The grime of Exodus
From the stone.
Only polished souls
Left the tomb:
Christ's locket
To Jerusalem
And now all
Creationdom.

At Pentecost
The Spirit
Had a lovefest
Knocking His
Espoused disciples
To the floor
While He set
The sky on fire
For His own banquet.

Around each neck
He encircled
A wedding band
Locket filled with
Rose petals and
Dove feathers.

The world in its
Golden chain from heaven
Hangs tonight
His glimmering
Locket of glory
Inscribed with
His love

For anyone
Whose heart
Has eyes—
Our locket within
His locket—
To reverence Him.

Amen.

My Perfect Lover

My whole life
I waited for
The perfect lover
I searched through
My dating youth, and
In early adulthood
And through a long, cold
Marriage. And even after
A more dry and brittle
Divorce I searched.

I interrogated friends,
Family, checkout clerks
To fix me up.
I went to bars, sat
Anxiously in church pews,
Looking, searching.
Around the running
Track I walked
Or hurried to catch up
With the right one just
Ahead of me. I went back
To the rolls of rejected
Former dates to see
If I was maybe

Too hasty, too select.
I could settle for one
Of these. Perfection maybe
Was too much to ask.

How many times had
Sympathetic mouths
Prophesied that there was
Someone out there.
No one called

Then when I gave up
Betrayed at last
By my own dreams
You came out
Of the Lamb's wool-white and soft
Wedding chapel
You had been
Preparing for us
Even before I
Entered the world
Of my mother's womb.
Thank you, Jesus.

Wedding Roses

Lord, thank you
For all the days
Of our lives
Like so many
Rose petals
You place
In the basket
Of our hands.

As we come
To know and
Love you more
You take a
Petal from us
And put it
In our path
Light from
Your garden's
Delight.

As you empty
Our basket
You fill your garden
Replacing our petals
With your roses.

Lord, why do we
Hoard petals
When you desire
To give us
The whole garden?
We strut with pied
Flimsy boutonnieres
When we could wear
A garland of halos.

We refuse your hand
Courting us with bounty
To decorate self
And divorce grace
Until even our petals
Shrivel into
Widow's weeds mourning over
A pained path of
Thistled elopements.

Lord, scatter may petals
Down the aisle
Of your coming
So I may carry
A bouquet of roses
In the bridal party
Of the Lamb.

A Litany for Christ

Christ here is
A litany
From the
Altar of my lips
Burning tonight
With coals of
Love for you:

Lord of life
Maker of time
God of the past
Ruler of the present
Overseer of the future
Steward of eternity
The Father's delight
Smile on angels' cheeks
Beauty's model
Prologue of peace
Endless beginnings
Glory of belief
Genesis of all.

Creations' Creator
Nature's law
Heaven's love

Sunrunner
Moonspinner
Star sculptor
Daystar's light
Joy of sunrise
Home of sunsets
Radiance in night
Inventor of motion
Carpenter of form
Artist of color
Master of molecules
Planner of planets
Earth's architect
Shepherd of fertility
Growth of grass
The call of couples
Rest of ages
Patriarch of humankind
Salvation Savior

Glory of creation
Light of time
King of Kyrie Eleisons
Perfection in flesh
Fulfillment of prophets
Keeper of hearts
Mender of dreams

Fountainhead of kindness
Assurance of mercy
Dismantler of walls
Chalice of cheer
Bread of bounty
Communion of saints
Victory of the cross
Triumph of resurrection
Christ, my all!

Union

O Daystar Christ
Wellspring of my delight
Enfold me in the
Resurrected soul
Of your sunrise
So that I am
Made gold by the alchemy
Of your light.

Wrap me in
Your loveliness
Let me feel the perfume of
Your breath, the winds,
Take me up
With you
Above the orchard clouds
Even farther than
The fertile loamed sky
Beyond the sight
Of any fields, spectacles
For the eyes of the mind.

Sweep me into
Your heart
Like a persimmon
You take off
The bough of life.
Enjoy me, O Lord,
For you created
All things of joy
And today my joy
Is created in you.

Make me a blanket
Out of your chamber music
So that I am

Wrapped in its air
As each note trebles
With the breath of the Trinity
Let me be a part
Of the particles your
Breath rushes through
In rushing love to the universe
Descending to me
So that I rise higher to thee.

Immerse me in all
The waters full of your
Reign above, below,
Within—an ark—calling me to
A tidal wave spilling
Over every created cell
Harboring a hope
Of seeing you.

Excite me
In the quiet roar
Of your spheres sailing
So fast you create
New planets before
The old ones cool. New
Earths and heavens
To adore and worship you.

At the end of this
Lovemaking
Let me feel
The tender release
Of you flooding
My ravished soul.

Jesus Fare

Jesus is
The pulley
From Heaven
To earth
Drawing us
Closer to
The Father.
As His
Word from
Heaven above
Gets taut
We start
To dance
In rhapsodic
Waltz air.
Slowly at
First then
Quicker than
Light shooting
Through angels.
We witness
Them travel
Jacob's ladder
Busy, bountiful
Grace messengers.
Then higher
All around
Spiroid stars
They touch
Ice blue
Red soft
Green supple
Until finally
Jesus pulls

Us into
God's lap
Up, up
And rest.

.

Bravissimo, Abba!

The Father's Love

… a candle
In the cold night
Light melting into warmth …

Pax

Like spinning tops
Where each striped color
Blends into one whirl
The orbs of God
Neither collide nor cease
But mark His passage
To each beating heart:

The body of Christ spinning
Within us His galaxy
Inside becoming outside
Outside turning inside
Christ's light sparkling
In our eyes of clay.

True peace flows from
One circle into another
From one heart to others
The cosmic Christ into
The molecules of our lives

The Trinity is
Omega into Alpha
Alpha into Omega
A top of many colors
A heart of pure white love.

Only when we begrudge the spin
Does the top stop.

The Soul

The soul is born
Before the body

It is birthed
In the Father's bosom

The sign of the soul
Is the spirit of light

You can see through it
All the sacraments

God's christening
Present to our future

The soul is
Freedom to love

Without time's
Wasteful haste

The soul is a cloud
Heaven's misty lining

It is a fine thread
Woven into altar cloth

The soul is the perfume
Of rain blossoming

Fruit in the desert
Spirit in the flesh

The Garden of Eden
Watered by Gethsemane

The soul is God's
Seal of faith

In our returning
Home to him

The soul is
A blanket of plenty

Nourishment for
That journey

Within it
God implants

The magnet to
Draw us to Him

A Psalm of the Sacraments

Baptize my heart, O Lord
So that it flows
With love and your mercy
Strength of babes.

Confirm my passage
Over and on the
Waters of the air
Your dominion of creation
Paths to you.

Lord, ordain my lips
To the priesthood of praise
Glorifying your name.
Consecrate my hands
To be lifted up

Higher and higher
To your heavens
Where no fowl dare fly
So I can play a
Psaltery in your stars.

Marry me, Lord,
To an angel
And crown the union
With glory and honor.

Anoint my tongue
With communion
On my first
And last voyage
Through an earthen vessel
To you.

Amen.

God's Playland

The journey through
Life to death
Is really quite
Short, a star's
Baby breath
In the long
Firmament of infinity—
Twinkling lullabies
Of Providence.

On the other side
Of time, eternity
Counts a different
Cadence, slow, slower
God turns back

Every clock
The world warred by.
Reversing the days,
Hours, minutes, seconds
Until time evaporates
And we are
The heir
Of God's playland
As He breathes
Everlasting life
Into us.

Without time
We are freed
From manacled frets
Holding us
In dust.
And like balloons
Kids release to
The skies
We belong
To Jesus
Like the
Breeze at Pentecost.

The Color of Wonder

God's world is
The color of wonder.

His sky is an
Umbrella that covers
Us with heaven.

The winds are
Prayer shawls draping

Us with breezes
Full of crocheted holiness.

The birds are
Small prayers,
Beads with wings
Litanies of the wind
Singing arias
Of air
In God's opera.

All the flowers
In the fields
Are shrines of spring
Patron saints of summer
Fortitude against winter.

The rivers are His
Dancing angels
Planting the land
With harmony
Furrowed with fertility,
A harvest of tomorrows.

Each of us is
A lamp filled
With sunlight
A light bulb
Christ turns on
Inside our face
Dust with golden souls
The sign of the cross
On the roads
Others travel
When they stop
Us for directions.

A Coronet of Words

And Father God
Saw the world
And showered
Love on it
The color of
Great crystal
Drops of precious
Gems and jewels
Raining such
Concelebrated
Majesty upon
His creation
That it
Glistened and
Reflected up
To the throne
From which
It came.

A star-speckled
Causeway
Came then
Traveled both
Up and down
Saints to heaven
Angels to earth
And with each journey
The glorious love
Of God
Shone brighter
Like a rainbow of
Amethysts, emeralds,
Alexandrites, rubies
Sapphires, opals,
And citrine
And all the jewels

From the throne
Room for earth
To see and hear
Diamond-size cuts
In the diadem of heaven
Rays of hope
And Father God
Saw the world
And showered
Love on it.

God's love
Always returns
To Him
A coronet
For the Word
And in our words.

The Vapors of God

My beloved's touch
Cools like the rains
Of spring upon
Mountain tops
He is high and
Lifts us holy
We are now in Him
As He is in us:
The gardener
Come to bed
In His garden.

Far above
The Father of Lights
Showers grace
So pure it comes

Only spun in air
From His nostrils...
Those whom He loves
Breathe in God's fragrance
Exhale transfiguration.

In the heart of God
There is such love
It overflows
Into the created
Universe of thought
Every idea of ours
Is a child of God
We are to raise
Up to Him
Pleasing in the generation.

God's love is
Fruitful forever
He lies down
With us in
A furrowing caress
And plenty rains
From His coming
Into the world
Every root feels
The excitement
Of the flower He
Impregnates in our soul:
The vapor of God
Restores.

On each tree
He weaves silver doves
That shine white
Like leaves in glory light
The fruit melts with taste
That we inhale.

Once you have
Tasted God and
Felt His pulse
Race through
The rows of your life
You'll be
Embedded with Him
Enfolded in His arms
Like grace notes
Fastened on to a
Sheet of music
Celebrating the
Sacred hymn.

Be open
To receive
The harvests
He wants
To compose
Inside of you.

Author God

God's love for us
Is a parable
Of our life
Perfected in Him

The greatest story
In the universe
Is God's
With us

Every journey
God makes with us
Is to Bethlehem
Or to Calvary

With visits
To Capernaum
In between

The people in
God's plot
Are always family
With the same last name:
Beth el Shaddai

All of us are
Hebrews in forever:
The call of the Father
Is in every tongue
Converted at Pentecost

The sights and
Wonders we behold
Are held in the
Palms of God

Creation is wisely
His present
Unfolding past
Into the eternal

When God reads us
He concludes
Our chapter
The instant
He composes it

He is the story
Teller of our lives
Narrator of mysteries
The author and finisher
Of every holy parable
We read in Him.

Yahweh Walking

On fertile plains
Yahweh walks
Sweetly with His people.

His feet plant
Roses in their souls.

The hem of His passing
Cures their thorns.

Now they are fresh-
Cut flowers for His altar.

The Bishop of Eternity

The Father is
The Bishop of eternity
The pastor of all
Souls going through
The gates of the Son
He shears woolly sheep
Into shining saints
Parishioners of the promise.

His crozier extends from
The Northern lights
To the Southern Cross
His cathedral is
The universe
His see starts
By planting us
In sacred soil
Flowered by the breath
Of the Spirit

Until acolyte angels
Carry us as fragrant
Rose petals
Placed on the
Father's altar throne
Celebrating His adoration.

The Father's Love

The Father's love
Is a candle
In the cold night
Light melting into warmth
A refuge in the wind
A town on a hill

The Father's love
Blankets the whole world
With stars and kindness
Sunlight and prophecy
The promise that
The pain won't last,
It just won't.

No one can ever
Escape His love
He is the East
And also the West
North and South
Are all one to Him
The polar caps tip
In homage to His love

The Father's love
Creates family
Out of strangers

He paints togetherness
Out of the gloom

There is no soul
Ever made who
Is not bred
In His image
We are twins
With Christ in His sight
Brothers and sisters
In the family of God

The Father's love
Is the hope
You can count on:
The first help
In your last
Desperate minutes

The Father's love
Is the song
You hear on
The radio that
Makes you
Cry for forgiveness.

It is the touch
Or spoken hug
You receive on
Days you feel
Isolated, convicted
To be in solitary
Confinement in the world.

The Father's love
Is the green
Light to go on
With your life

When the world shouts:
No

The Father's love
Leads to a prayer
Unlike any ever
Said aloud in a church
It is a doxology
Of our close
Relationship to Abba
A secret so intimate
We can trust
Only Him with it.

The Father's love
Never stops
Even when we
Think it might
Or should

It goes on.

Philip C. Kolin is a professor of English at the University of Southern Mississippi, Hattiesburg. A graduate of Chicago State University and the University of Chicago, he received his doctorate from Northwestern University. He has written more than twenty books and countless articles on Shakespeare, Tennessee Williams, Edward Albee, and other authors. His most recent book, on the production and cultural history of A Streetcar Named Desire, was published by Cambridge University Press in its Plays in Production series.

Philip Kolin is an authority on technical and business writing; his Successful Writing at Work (Houghton Mifflin) is in its sixth edition. He has received many honors and research grants, and in 1991–93 he was Charles W. Moorman Alumni Distinguished Professor in the Humanities at the University of Southern Mississippi. He was founding coeditor of Studies in American Drama, 1945–Present, published by Ohio State University Press and recognized by the Conference of Editors of Learned Journals as the best new journal of 1986.

Philip Kolin's poetry has appeared in Christianity and Literature, Living Streams, Xavier Review, Silver Wings, Channels, the Michigan Quarterly Review, the South Carolina Review, the Anglican Theological Review, and other journals. His Roses for Sharron: Poems was published by Colonial Press in 1993. Deep Wonder is his first book entirely devoted to religious poetry.

Philip Kolin is a member of St. Thomas Aquinas Parish in Hattiesburg.

———— To Order Additional Copies of **Deep Wonder** ————

Please send check or money order to:
 Grey Owl Press
 P.O. Box 5334
 Takoma Park MD 20913
 (Price: $12.95; D.C. residents please add $0.75 sales tax per copy)

or order through our Website:
 www.greyowlpress.com

or call:
 1-800-431-1579

or order through:
 www.amazon.com
 www.bn.com

———— Also Available from **Grey Owl Press** ————

Lion Sun: Poems by Pavel Chichikov
$12.95. 96 pages. ISBN 0-9671901-0-X

Lion Sun brings together more than 70 poems by a Catholic author who takes his inspiration from the splendor and terror of the natural world. The book includes six illustrations by Illinois artist Eric Young, who also created the cover image.

… one feels that glory and mystery are lurking in every line …
 Thomas Howard, professor of English at St. John's Seminary,
 Brighton, Massachusetts

This book is set in Goudy Old Style, designed in 1915 by Frederic W. Goudy for American Type Founders. Flexible enough for both text and display, it is one of the most popular typefaces ever produced. Its recognizable features include the diamond-shaped dots on the letters i and j and on punctuation marks, the upturned ear of the g, and the bases of the letters E and L. Several years later, in response to the overwhelming popularity of Cooper Black, Lanston Monotype commissioned Goudy to design heavy versions of Goudy Old Style. Goudy Heavyface and Goudy Heavyface Italic were released in 1925.

The huge success of Goudy's typefaces led to the addition of several weights to many of his typefaces. Designers working for American Type Founders produced additions to the family. In 1927, Morris Fuller Benton drew Goudy Extra Bold.

The ornaments are in the font ITC Cancione, developed by calligrapher and illustrator Brenda Walton. Taking her inspiration from fourth-century Roman inscriptions, Walton gave ITC Cancione a slender, elegant, high-waisted form, with the thick-and-thin variation of brushstrokes on stone. She heightened the effect by adding a rough texture to the letters, as though they had been rubbed from a weatherworn façade. Walton, who lives in northern California, focuses mainly on developing hand lettering and illustrations for gift collections, book jackets, and business identities. One of her specialties is designing collections featuring botanical illustrations. It is not surprising that ITC Cancione includes a large number of floral ornaments and tendril-like flourishes, each showing the flowing forms of brushwork, but roughened and weathered.